OCEAN TIDES AND TSUNAMIS

NATURE BOOK FOR KIDS

Children's Nature Books

BABY PROFESSOR
EDUCATION KIDS

Speedy Publishing LLC
40 E. Main St. #1156
Newark, DE 19711
www.speedypublishing.com

When you visit the ocean, you can see the water is usually in motion. There are waves lapping and splashing, and there may a line where the dry sand turns to wet sand. Why is the ocean so active? Read on and learn about two of the biggest activities in ocean water: tides and tsunamis!

Waves

THE TIDE IS FROM SPACE!

Most of the movement of the surface of the sea is waves. Waves are caused in part by the wind and by the action of ocean currents. But the by far the biggest wave action in the sea is the tide.

Twice a day the ocean's water moves toward its highest point on the shore, and twice a day it retreats toward its lowest point. What causes this movement is the gravitational force of our moon and the sun.

Every body exerts gravitational force on every other body. You experience this every day, as the Earth's gravitation pulls you down toward the center of the planet and keeps you from just continuing to float away from the ground when you jump.

It also explains why you fall so very fast when you slip: gravity is pulling on you all the time, and as soon as you are not balanced over your legs (or your hands, if you are doing a handstand!), the Earth hauls you down with a bang! Read more about gravity in the Baby Professor book *Can I Dance on the Moon?*

Earth's gravity has a strong effect on you, the air, and the water of our planet. But both the moon and the sun have gravitation pull on everything on the Earth's surface. This effect is most obvious with our oceans.

North winds on waves.

SPRING TIDE

TIDE TYPES OF EARTH

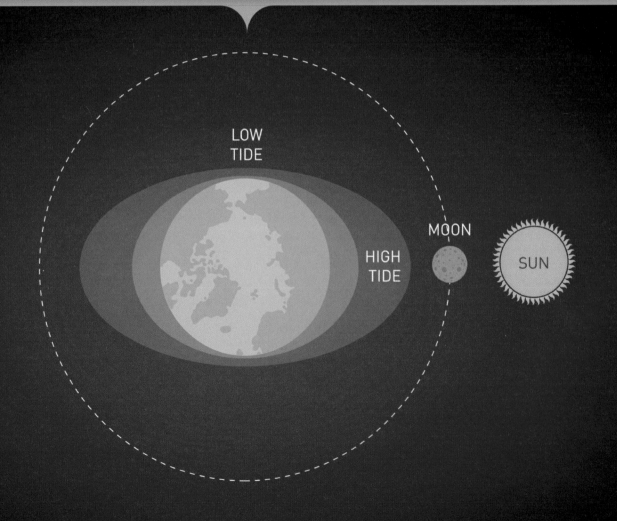

LOW
TIDE

HIGH
TIDE

MOON

SUN

SPRING TIDE

Since the moon is closer to us, its gravitation effect is greater than the sun's. On the side of the Earth facing the moon, the water in the oceans bulges up slightly in response to the gravitational pull and the water comes in along the shore to make *"High Tide"*. On the side of the Earth not facing the moon, the water moves away from the shore to make *"Low Tide"*. This happens roughly twice a day.

The sun has a similar, smaller effect. When the moon and the sun are on opposite sides of the Earth, the gravitation forces partly cancel each other out, and both high and low tides are less extreme This is called a **Neap Tide.** And when the moon is on the same side of the Earth as the sun, the tides can get to their greatest highs and lows.

NEAP TIDE

TIDE TYPES OF EARTH

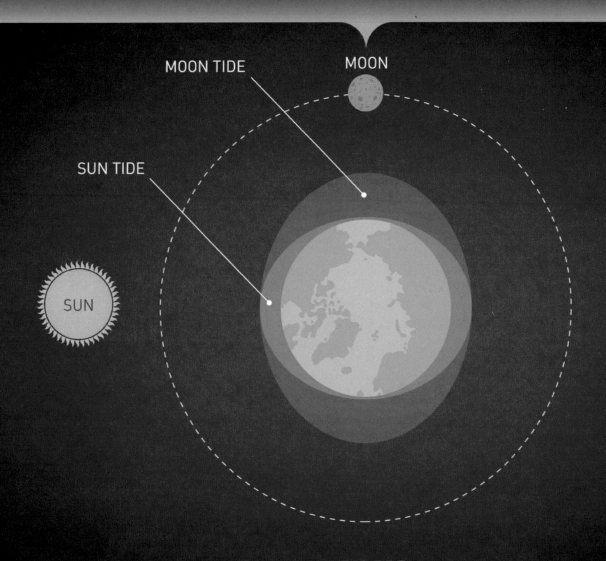

MOON TIDE

MOON

SUN TIDE

SUN

NEAP TIDE

Hopewell Rock in the Bay of Fundy at low tide

HIGH TIDES IN THE BAY OF FUNDY

The shape of the shoreline and how shallow part of the ocean is also affect the size of the tides. The highest tidal range in the world is in the Bay of Fundy, between New Brunswick and Nova Scotia in eastern Canada. The Bay is much more shallow than the open ocean, and is shaped like a narrow, long bottle. This exaggerates the tidal effect, so at its most extreme the difference between high and low tide can reach over fifty feet!

St. Martins Sea Caves High Tide.

The extreme tide change in the Bay of Fundy speeds erosion, creating sharp cliffs. The erosion releases lots of nutrients into the water, attracting fish, whales, and other marine life. Several projects are under way to try to harness the power of the Bay of Fundy tides to create electrical energy, without hurting the Bay's ecosystem.

The high tides often provide a surprise for visiting sailors. You may anchor your boat in ten feet of water, row to shore for supplies, and then find, when you return, that your boat is lying on its side on a mud flat!

High tide in the Bay of Fundy.

Freak wave on ocean, Tsunami waves.

A TSUNAMI FOLLOWS A HUGE EVENT

"Tsunami" is Japanese for *"Harbor Wave"*. It is the general term for these events, even though the waves affect whole coastlines, not just harbors. It probably arose because fishermen, out on the sea, would not notice the tsunami waves passing under them, as the waves only pile up as they get to shallow water. Then, when the fisherme got home, they might find their harbour and their village mysteriously devastated.

While tides are regular, predictable events, tsunamis are not. A tsunami is a series of large waves caused by some disturbance in the ocean. The disturbance could be an earthquake, a volcanic eruption, a meteor hitting the ocean, a landslide, an underwater explosion, or some other major event.

Stormy wave.

G reek scientists first suggested that tsunamis were caused by undersea earthquakes over two thousand years ago, but they are still mysterious. For example, scientists do not yet know why some earthquakes create tsunamis, and some do not.

Giant blue waves crested with foam.

Water does not compress. This means that when a force acts on it, water gets pushed in the direction ("along the vector") of the force. When an event creates force that creates waves, the waves can travel hundreds of miles across the open ocean and arrive with little warning at a shore far away from the originating event.

Tsunami wave coming to city

Powerful Breaking Wave.

TSUNAMI WAVES

When a tsunami is coming, first the ocean may seem to draw away from the shore. Then a series of large waves comes in, sometimes sending huge amounts of water long distances inland. The waves of a tsunami usually arrive in a series, a *"Wave Train"*, with each wave minutes or hours apart from the next one. Each wave can be as much as thirty feet high.

Tsunami waves don't look like regular waves; they look more like the tide coming in—but much, much higher and faster than normal. This is why they are sometimes called **Tidal Waves,** even though tsunami waves have nothing to do with the tide.

Colorful Ocean Peak.

LANDSLIDES

Underwater landslides can create huge tsunamis as they displace large volumes of water very quickly. In 1958, a landslide in Alaska generated the highest wave ever recorded: 1700 feet high! Fortunately, the landslide and wave were in a bay, which contained its destructive force.

A similar event in the waters of the Vajont Dam in Italy caused a wave surge over 800 feet high that killed over two thousand people.

Longarone (BL) after Vajont disaster dam, 1963.

Cinematic Portrayal of a City Destroyed by Tsunami.

TSUNAMI DISASTERS

Tsunamis can cause extensve death and destruction. Since 1850, over 400,000 people have died because of tsunamis.

Tsunamis have two chances to cause damage. The first is when the walls of water travelling at high speed smash into land, buildings, and forests. The second is when the water drains back into the sea, carrying wreckage with it. Smashed trees and parts of buildings can cause damage on their way down to the sea to structures that may have survived the waves as they came in.

Here are some tsunami disasters from the recent past and from long ago.

INDONESIA, 2004

A giant earthquake near Indonesia set off a huge tsunami that killed over 200,000 people in countries around the Indian Ocean.

A village near the coast of Sumatra lays in ruin after the Tsunami that struck South East Asia.

FUKUSHIMA, 2011

Japan's nuclear reactors at Fukushima were protected by high sea walls along 15 miles of shoreline. When the tsunami waves rolled in, they were 50% higher than the walls, and just spilled over them and knocked many of the walls down. This was a disaster all along the coast, but particularly in that it caused a massive spill of radiocatve material at the reactor.

Damage scenery of the East Japan great earthquake disaster.

ALEXANDRIA, 365

A tsunami heavily damaged Alexandria in Egypt in 365. Historian Ammianus Marcellinus is the first to have recorded the pattern of an earthquake, the sea drawing back from the shore, and then the huge waves rolling in and damaging the shore and the city.

MESSINA, 1908

This earthquake and resulting tsunami caused more than 100,000 deaths, and was one of the worst natural disasters in Europe in recorded history.

THE STOREGGA SLIDE, 6,000 BCE

In the North Sea between England and Denmark there was once a large, low territory that historians call Doggerland. It was inhabited, and the southern part of it linked Britain to what is now France. About eight thousand years ago there were three huge landslides in Norway involving almost 200 miles of cliffs.

The landslides triggered a disastrous tsunami that changed the British coastline, eliminated Doggerland altogether, changing it to a shallow part of the North Sea, and killed all its inhabitants, an unknown number of people.

Tsunamai Hazard

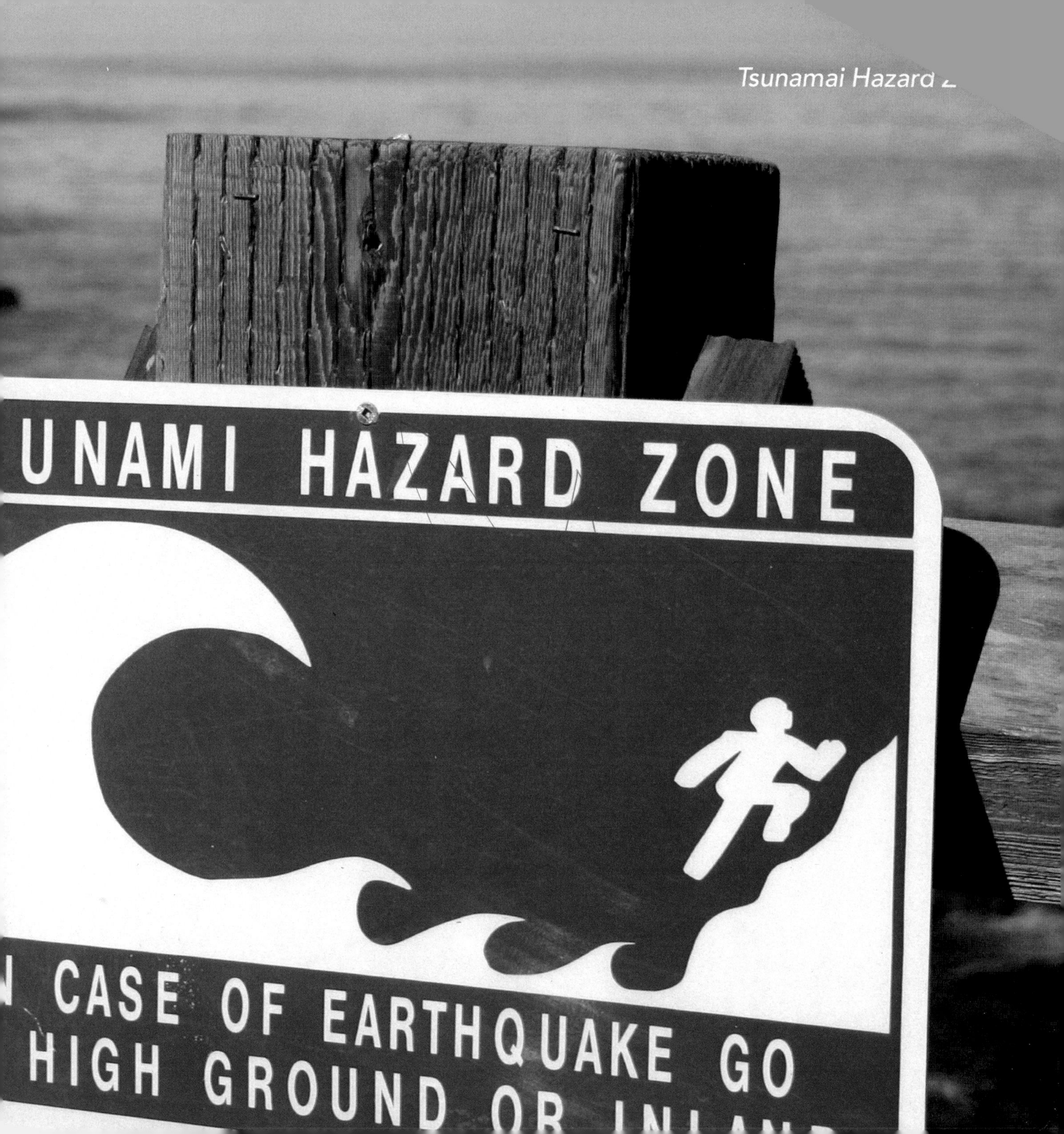

TSUNAMI WARNINGS

We can't predict tsunamis, but once one happens, we can send out warnings. Sensors attached to buoys in the Pacific and Indian oceans record pressure changes in the water and send out a signal when it looks like a tsunami is happening. The signal goes to warning stations on vulnerable shores which may help some people escape.

It may be too late to get out of the way once you see a tsunami coming, as the waves travel at more than 400 miles per hour.

   In 2004 Tilly Smith, aged ten, was on a beach in Thailand with her parents. She noticed the water drawing back very quickly and, remembering what she had learned in school, warned her parents. Her family and dozens of other people managed to escape the tsunami by fleeing immediately.

Tsunami evacuation route sign.

LEARN MORE ABOUT THE EARTH

Our Earth provides a safe for us home most of the time. But things can get dangerous and deadly. Read other Baby Professor books, like *What Happens Before and After Volcanoes Erupt?* and *A Kid's Book of Extreme Weather*, to learn more about dangers to look out for.

Visit

BABY PROFESSOR
EDUCATION KIDS

www.BabyProfessorBooks.com

to download Free Baby Professor eBooks
and view our catalog of new and exciting
Children's Books

Made in the USA
Middletown, DE
09 August 2021